Advanced Market Structure

Market mastery unveiled: navigating the
depths of advanced market structures for
financial success

Abraham Robert. C

This book comes with a link that grants you unique access to a complimentary video version, which will enhance your reading experience by adding a visual learning element.

Get the access link at the end of this book

TABLE OF CONTENT

*Chapter 6*_____ *93*

Market structure in different time frame _____**93**

Chapter 1

Foundation of market structure

Understanding Price action

The discipline of basing all of your trading choices on a "naked," or simplified, price chart is known as price action trading. With the possible exception of a few moving averages to help identify dynamic support and resistance regions and trends, this means that there are no trailing indicators.

Price charts are used by all financial markets to show statistics on how a market's price has changed over different time periods.

The opinions and behaviors of all participants (human or machine) in a market over a certain time period are reflected in price charts, and these behaviors are represented as price action on a market's price chart.

Although economic statistics and other worldwide news events serve as market catalysts, we don't need to examine them in order to trade the market profitably. The explanation is really straightforward: price action on a market's price chart is the final reflection of any economic data and global news that influences price movement inside a market.

Using lagging price indicators, such as stochastics, MACD, RSI, and others, is a complete waste of time because a market's price movement reflects all factors influencing that market for any given period of time. All the signs you'll ever need to create a winning, high-probability trading strategy are found in price movement.

These signals, taken as a whole, are referred to as price action trading techniques. They offer a means of understanding the price movement of a market and aid in making accurate enough predictions about its future movement to provide you with a high-probability trading strategy.

The Price Action Trading System

The majority of methods typically feature a two-step procedure for locating and seizing trading opportunities in the market, making price action trading a straightforward approach. The following are the steps to follow:

1. Determine the prevailing market circumstances

A market may be in an uptrend, decline, or sideways movement, as was previously described. Traders should be able to determine the stage of price action the market is in at any one time by just looking at asset prices.

2. Determine the Trading Possibility

A trader first determines the current state of the market before determining whether there is a viable trading opportunity. For example, in an uptrend, the trader should be able to determine from the market movement whether a retracement is anticipated or if prices will continue to extend higher.

Price Action Indicators

For a price action trader, price and time are the only relevant trade elements. Because of this, a price chart is a price action trader's most valuable trading tool. Because of their esthetic attractiveness and the comprehensive information they provide traders with regarding asset prices, candlestick charts are the most often used on practically all platforms.

The high, low, opening, and closing prices (HLOC) of an asset over a certain time period are shown on a typical candlestick. On most platforms, a candle that closes at a higher price than it opened at is labeled as bullish (green), whereas a candle that closes at a lower price than it opened at is labeled as bearish (red).

A price action trader can learn a great deal about the aggregate behavior of market players from this comprehensive pricing data.

The size, shape, and information that a price action trader can obtain from a candle are all determined by the placement of HLOC price points. Because of this, certain types of candles offer neutral signs like Doji, bearish signals like hanging man, and bullish ones like hammer.

A chart is printed with several candlesticks over time, candlestick patterns appear on the chart, and this provides price action traders with more pricing information.

When properly comprehended and interpreted, candlestick patterns enable traders to follow the rise and fall of market waves and identify profitable price action possibilities. Price action traders use clean charts to trade because they can read candlesticks and chart patterns.

Three main signals are provided to traders by various chart patterns: continuation, reversal, or neutral.

Neutral patterns, like symmetrical triangles, can form in any market and while they signal that a big move is about to happen, they do not provide a directional cue. Continuation patterns, like directional wedges and flags, form in trending markets and signal that the dominant trend will continue.

Reversal patterns, like head and shoulders and double bottoms, signal that the momentum of the prevailing trend is fading and a reversal is about to happen.

It is more crucial to understand and analyze the information provided by candlesticks and chart patterns than it is to commit their construction to memory. To ascertain the market's price trajectory, pay attention to the candlesticks. Price action traders can use Trend-lines in addition to candles and candlestick patterns to determine the best times to enter and exit the market.

Trading Strategies Using Price Action

Price action tactics entail observing fluctuations in market prices to gain insight into the psychology of market participants. Here are a few of the market's most dependable price movement setups:

Candles with Long Wicks

In the market, a body and wick(s) represent a candle. The wicks show the extremes, or the high and low reached, whilst the body indicates the difference between the opening and closing values. A popular choice among price action traders are candles with long wicks. A candle with a long upper wick, for example, indicates that during that time, sellers fought attempts by buyers to drive prices higher and even succeeded in bringing prices back to the opening price.

With this knowledge, a price action trader can either wait for confirmation or support the selling once more in the next period. Long wick candles are a must-watch for price action traders in any case.

Inside Bar After Breakouts

Traders are faced with the issue of determining whether a breakout is real or fake. The term "inside" refers to a pattern of breakout where one or more candles trade within the highs and lows of the huge breakout candle. The psychology behind the setup is that market players are prepared to support and defend the new trend moving ahead and are hesitant to give up any breakout gains.

Trend-line Trading

Using lines to determine the best times to enter trades in trending markets is known as trend-line trading.

A trend-line is drawn from one swing low to the next in an uptrend, and it is then projected forward in time. An excellent moment to enter the upswing is during retracements to the trend-line. In a variety of markets, horizontal trend-lines can be used to plot regions of support and resistance.

The role of volume in market structure

Volume is a crucial factor in trading activity analysis that should not be disregarded. Volume is the total number of shares or contracts that are traded in a specific market or security over a specific time frame. It is essential to technical analysis because it offers insightful information about the direction and intensity of price changes.

Using volume to confirm Price Movements: Volume serves as a price movement confirming indicator.

Higher trading volume and price gains during an uptrend indicate strong purchasing demand and an optimistic outlook. On the other hand, low trading volume during price falls could be an indication of weak selling pressure or even a reversal of the trend. By examining volume in addition to price changes, traders can increase their confidence in a trend's authenticity.

Using volume to confirm Trend Reversals: Trend reversals may be detected with the aid of volume. A sharp increase in trading volume followed by a big decline in price could portend an impending turnaround. Volume climaxes are a common indicator that market sentiment is changing, and traders should be on the lookout for potential trend reversals.

Using volume to evaluate Market Strength: Volume analysis can shed light on the market's general strength.

A strong bullish feeling and widespread market involvement are indicated when prices are rising on heavy volume. On the other hand, a big volume of decreasing prices suggests that there is widespread selling pressure and a negative attitude.

Trades can be made with confidence by evaluating the strength of the market by measuring the volume that accompanies price swings.

Divergence Signals: When the price and volume indicators move against one other, this is known as volume divergence. A trend reversal may be indicated, for instance, if prices are rising but volume is declining. This could signal waning buying desire.

On the other hand, decreasing prices combined with rising volume could indicate a strengthening selling pressure and possible trend continuance. Volume divergences can give traders important information about potential changes in market sentiment.

Comparing Volume Patterns: Traders might find possible breakouts or breakdowns by examining volume patterns. A stock that is consolidating inside a small range and experiencing a decline in volume, for instance, can be a sign of hesitation. When the stock breaks out of this zone, volume may spike sharply, which might be a strong indicator of a possible upward move. An improved knowledge of market dynamics can be attained by traders by analyzing volume patterns before and after notable price events.

Market Size and Volume: The volume offers information on the liquidity and depth of the market. In general, a market with a higher trading volume is thought to be more liquid and offer more options for buying and selling. A market like this allows traders to enter and exit positions with ease, reducing the possibility of slippage and guaranteeing effective trade execution.

Evaluation of Risk: Analyzing volume can help determine the level of market risk. Unexpected increases in volume during periods of price falls or rises could be a symptom of greater volatility, elevated uncertainty, or the occurrence of noteworthy news events. Volume information is a useful tool for traders to modify their risk management plans.

Volume is an essential part of technical analysis and provides insightful information about the behavior of the market. Traders can verify trends, find divergence signals, evaluate market strength, identify reversals, and analyze volume patterns by examining volume in conjunction with price changes.

Comprehending the importance of volume and integrating it into your trading approach will augment your ability to make decisions and potentially yield better trading results.

Chapter 2

Support and resistance: the pillar of market structure

Support and Resistance

Support and resistance (S&R) levels, also known as SNR in Forex, are a fundamental component of technical analysis (TA). The field of technical analysis is based on price data patterns, and S&R plays an important part.

Support and resistance refer to price levels when prices change direction or move sideways.

In other words, S&R refers to a price level or zone where the price has bounced.

Support Levels:

• Are always found lower the current price.

• Indicate purchasing pressure.

• Provide a potential bullish bouncing point or break breakout.

Resistance Levels:

• Always found above the current pricing.

• Indicate selling pressure.

• Identify a probable bearish bounce point or positive breakout.

Important of Support and Resistance Levels

Support and resistance (S&R) levels are an important aspect of any market analysis or chart for a variety of reasons.

• The market employs S&R levels to identify breakouts and bounces.

• S&R is used by technical analysts, bank traders, and fund managers.

• Universal: they appear across all instruments and time contexts.

• Market phases occur during trends, ranges, and reversals.

• Higher time frames are more relevant as they are used by a broader market segment.

Support and resistance levels resemble the "footprints" of major market players. S&R analysis can help other traders better understand their moves.

Benefit of S&R in trading

Support and resistance lines are an important feature of trading and understanding market structure (see paragraph above). Without it, traders would be lost in the woods, as if they were driving blindfolded down the road.

The three primary benefits of S&R

1. Detecting high probability reversal zones.

2. Avoid low-probability transactions in S&R.

3. Trade setups for S&R break or bounce.

Mistakes traders make while drawing S&R on a chart

Mistake 1: They expect a support level to remain supportive even after the price has broken below the level or zone.

The same is true for resistance when price has burst through it. Traders should watch for unbroken support and resistance levels.

Mistake 2: They employ levels from a long time ago. Always remember that the most recent price movement carries more weight and importance.

Mistake 3: They regard all S&R levels same. Support and resistance levels become more critical if the price has previously bounced strongly at this level. So, start on the right and work your way back to the left.

Mistake 4: They believe that trading every S&R level is the best way to go. The truth is that this results in a disorganized chart that does more harm than good. Concentrate on only drawing significant S&R values.

Drawing support and resistance level

The primary step is to look for recent S&R levels that have been "respected". The market bounces at a support and resistance level. The greater the bounce, the more potent the S&R level becomes.

Another idea is to create a "zone" rather than a single level, as price momentum and market volatility might cause price to overshoot S&R. We employ these buffer zones for S&R on all tools and indicators, including moving averages, where we prefer to deal with moving average bands (high, low, and close) rather than a single moving average.

Also, do not be hesitant to highlight variations in S&R levels. Some S&R levels will be more essential than others, therefore it is useful to categorize S&R as major or minor. The ideal method is to use different shades of color for the S&R lines.

Liquidity pools

Liquidity pools are an important and dynamic component of the Forex market, representing the overall availability of currencies for trade at any one time. They play a critical role in determining market characteristics, impacting pricing, execution speed, and overall market stability.

Understanding liquidity pools is critical for Forex traders and investors since they have a direct impact on trading performance and risk management.

Liquidity pools, also known as "liquidity," include all buy and sell orders placed by market participants in the Forex market.

These orders are combined among multiple brokers, financial institutions, and trading platforms to establish a large pool of currencies accessible for trade. Liquidity pools show the depth of the market by indicating the amount of money accessible at various price levels.

Key Features of Liquidity Pools:

Price impact:

The depth of liquidity at various price levels influences price movements. Price movements are typically lower and more consistent in locations with high liquidity (a large number of buy and sell orders). Price swings can be more pronounced in places with reduced liquidity.

Execution Speed:

Liquidity pools influence the speed with which orders are executed. Orders in high liquidity areas are often filled fast since there are numerous players prepared to buy or sell at the current pricing. Low liquidity might cause slower order execution as it takes longer to find matching orders.

Bid/Ask Spread:

The bid-ask spread is the difference between the greatest price a buyer is willing to pay (the bid) and the lowest amount a seller would take (the ask). Liquidity pools determine the width of the spread; increased liquidity frequently results in reduced spreads, lowering trading costs for participants.

Market orders versus limit orders:

Traders can create two sorts of orders: market orders and limit orders. Market orders are performed immediately at the current market price, whereas limit orders are set at predetermined price levels and executed when the market hits those levels. Liquidity pools determine which counterparties are available to fill limit orders.

The importance of liquidity pools:

Understanding the dynamics of liquidity pools is important for various reasons.

Risk Management:

Liquidity pools provide information about market depth and potential price slippage. Traders can measure liquidity at different price levels to efficiently manage their risk. In illiquid markets, significant price slippage can occur when large orders are executed, affecting trading outcomes.

Trade execution:

Traders use knowledge about liquidity pools to select the best entry and exit points.

They seek to execute orders in locations with high liquidity in order to reduce slippage and trading expenses. Timing is critical in completing orders at favorable prices.

Market Stability:

Liquidity pools help to maintain market stability by ensuring there are enough buyers and sellers available. High liquidity levels tend to smooth out market movements, lowering the likelihood of dramatic price spikes or crashes.

Market Analysis:

Liquidity levels are frequently examined by forex analysts while doing technical and fundamental research. Changes in liquidity can provide useful information about market sentiment and potential turning points.

Forex Supply and Demand Zones

Forex supply and demand zones are chart locations where currency pair prices are anticipated to fluctuate due to buyer-seller imbalances. These zones emerge when there is a considerable increase in purchasing or selling pressure. Traders utilize them to anticipate price reversals and continuations.

In forex trading, price movements are determined by supply and demand. High demand (more buyers than sellers) raises prices, while oversupply (more sellers than buyers) brings them down. This principle is crucial in trading.

All marketable assets eventually achieve equilibrium, resulting in supply and demand zones. These zones are price pauses that occur while the market balances between buyers and sellers. Traders use this notion to locate trading opportunities.

Economic policies, political events, and market mood all have an impact on forex supply and demand. For example, when the US raises interest rates, demand for the US dollar may increase as investors seek higher yields. Political turbulence or wars, on the other hand, may impede international investment, limiting foreign currency supply and increasing the US dollar's exchange rate.

Key Steps to Identify Supply and Demand Zones

Identifying supply and demand follows the same method as identifying support and resistance levels. However, there are still a few little distinctions between the two.

Here are the measures you should take to recognize these zones like a pro:

1. Identify major price levels on the chart, including highs and lows.

2. Identify price consolidation or ranging areas on the chart over time. These zones are frequently associated with a supply-demand equilibrium.

3. Price spikes might suggest a sudden rise in buying or selling pressure, resulting in a zone of supply or demand.

4. Apply technical analysis indicators. These tools can assist you in identifying places or zones where prices may recover, as well as creating supply or demand zones.

5. Follow market news and announcements from central bankers to learn about any specific FX levels that local banks may preserve.

The Demand Zone

A demand zone is a specific location on a price chart that is marked by strong buying activity, resulting in either a price rise or a reversal of a downward trend. Identifying a demand zone entails evaluating chart locations where the price has consistently rebounded, indicating buyers' readiness to participate in the market at that level.

In actuality, forex market players frequently make trades at this price level or abandon short-selling positions because they identify it as a significant price point that will be difficult to breach.

Supply Zone

A supply zone is a distinct sector on a price chart that is marked by significant selling pressure, resulting in either a price decrease or a reversal of an upward trend.

Identifying supply zones entails looking at price levels where multiple attempts to breach have met resistance, indicating increased selling pressure.

Chapter 3

Trend analysis: identifying market direction

Market Trend:

A market trend is a fundamental concept in finance and investment that represents the overall direction in which asset or security prices move over a given time period. Understanding market trends is critical for investors, traders, and analysts because it provides the foundation for making informed judgments in financial markets.

A market trend is the general direction in which asset or security prices move within a particular market or financial instrument over time.

Various market trends

Some of the most common forms of market trends:

Uptrend (Bull market): Asset prices often increase over time. This trend is distinguished by a sequence of higher highs and higher lows. Bull markets are frequently connected with increased investor confidence, economic expansion, and optimism.

Downtrend (Bear market) Asset prices often decline over time. This trend is characterized by a series of lower highs and lows. Bear markets are frequently associated with negative attitudes, economic downturns, and pessimism.

Sideways or range-bound trend: Asset prices move within a limited price range without a definite upward or downward trend.

Prices typically fluctuate within a limited range, indicating a lack of strong confidence among investors, resulting in a time of consolidation.

Factors influencing market trends:

1. Economic Data

2. Corporate earnings.

3. Monetary policy

4. Geopolitical developments

5. Market sentiment.

6. Supply and Demand Dynamics

Economic data: including GDP growth, unemployment, inflation, and consumer mood, have a considerable impact on market patterns. Positive economic data can fuel bullish patterns, but bad data might exacerbate bearish tendencies.

Corporate earnings: The financial performance of publicly traded companies significantly impacts market patterns. Strong profit reports can bolster bullish movements, whilst negative earnings might fuel bearish trends.

Central banks: monetary policy actions affect interest rates and liquidity in the financial sector. Interest rate and monetary policy changes can have an impact on market patterns, notably in bonds and currencies.

Geopolitical events: such as international conflicts and trade disputes, can cause uncertainty in financial markets, leading to fluctuations in attitude and patterns. Geopolitical stability can encourage bullish trends, whilst geopolitical tensions might exacerbate bearish tendencies.

Market sentiment: Investors, traders, and institutions can influence market developments.

Positive sentiment can generate buying pressure and bullish movements, whilst negative feeling can generate selling pressure and bearish trends.

Supply and demand: Market developments are driven by the supply-demand balance for assets. When demand exceeds supply, prices typically rise, resulting in uptrends. In contrast, when supply exceeds demand, prices tend to decline, resulting in downward trends.

Importance of keeping track on market trends

Here's why market trends are so crucial to keep track of.

1. Decision-making.

2. Risk management.

3. Timing.

4. Develop strategy

5. Diversify portfolio

6. Long-term investment

Decision-making: Market trends help investors and traders make informed judgments. Understanding the prevalent trend can help you decide whether to buy, sell, or hold an item.

Risk management: Effective risk management requires an understanding of market patterns. Traders and investors can use trend analysis to alter their positions and execute risk mitigation methods.

Timing: Market trends can assist traders and investors in better timing their entry and exit strategies. Buying in an uptrend and selling in a slump might increase the likelihood of profitable trades.

Develop strategy: Developing trading and investment strategies requires a strong understanding of trends. Trend-following, trend reversal, and range-bound tactics all rely on identifying market trends.

Diversifying portfolios: Using trend research allows investors to diversify across asset classes or sectors with various tendencies. Spreading the risk can be aided by this diversity.

Long-term investment: Long-term investment involves detecting and tracking important market patterns to accumulate wealth over time. Investing in assets that are consistent with long-term bullish trends can be a wise strategy.

How do you recognize market trends

Here are some popular strategies for identifying market trends:

Price Analysis

•Drawing trend-lines on a pricing chart can aid in identifying patterns. In an uptrend, connect higher lows; in a downtrend, connect lower highs. Support and resistance levels are also provided by trend-lines.

• Moving averages smooth price data and identify trends. The most frequent types are the Simple Moving Average (SMA) and the Exponential Moving Average (EMA). Prices above a moving average may suggest an uptrend, while prices below it may signal a downturn.

• Price patterns, including head and shoulders, double tops, and flags, can indicate trend reversals or continuations.

• The relative strength index (RSI) assesses the pace and amount of price movements. An RSI number greater than 70 may indicate an overbought condition and a potential trend reversal, whereas an RSI less than 30 may indicate an oversold condition and a possible uptrend reversal.

• Moving average convergence divergence (MACD) is a momentum indicator that detects changes in trend direction.

• The average directional index (ADX) indicates the strength of a trend. A rising ADX implies a strong trend, whilst a falling ADX could indicate a deteriorating trend.

Volume Analysis

Consider examining trade volume alongside price fluctuations. In an uptrend, higher volume during price rises might reinforce the trend's strength. Rising volume during falls can suggest that a slump is likely to continue.

Fundamental Analysis

Consider basic market drivers including economic statistics, corporate results, and news events. Positive economic statistics and excellent earnings may help to fuel an uptrend, whilst unfavorable news and economic downturns may contribute to a downward trend.

Steps for conducting market trend analysis:

1. Collect data

2. Select a timeframe.

3. Create price charts.

4. Identify trends.

5. Use trend-lines.

6. Apply moving averages.

7. Use technical indicators.

8. Look for chart trends.

9. Analyze Volume

10. Fundamental Analysis

Collect data: Gather historical pricing data for the asset or market you want to investigate.

You can get this information via financial websites, trading platforms, and data suppliers.

Choose a timeframe: to analyze. Common timeframes are daily, weekly, and monthly. Your trading or investing horizon determines which timeframe you use.

Create price charts with historical data: Line charts, candlestick charts, and bar charts are popular chart types. Select the one that best suits your analysis style.

Identify trends: Analyze price data to identify patterns. In an uptrend (bull market), watch for higher highs and higher lows, while in a downturn (bear market), look for lower highs and lower lows.

Use trend-lines: to identify trend direction and intensity. Connect the lows in an uptrend to the highs in a decline.

Trend-lines can function as both support and resistance levels.

Use moving averages: (e.g., Simple or Exponential) to smooth price data and spot trends. Prices above a moving average may suggest an uptrend, while prices below it may signal a downturn.

Use technical indicators: to confirm trends and evaluate their strength. Common indicators include the relative strength index (RSI), moving average convergence divergence (MACD), and average directional index (ADX).

Identify chart patterns: including head and shoulders, double tops/bottoms, flags, and triangles. These patterns can help predict whether a trend will reverse or continue.

Analyze trading volume and price variations: Increasing volume during price gains might reinforce a trend's strength, whilst declining volume may indicate a fading trend.

Consider economic indicators: earnings reports, and news events while conducting fundamental research. These variables can support or refute your trend analysis.

How do market trends work

Here's how market trends work:

1. Price fluctuations.

2. Market sentiment.

3. Fundamental Factors

4. Technical Analysis

5. Market Participants.

6. News and Events

Price fluctuations: Market trends mostly depend on asset price changes. An uptrend occurs when prices are generally rising, whereas a downtrend occurs when prices are generally decreasing. Price movements can be impacted by a variety of factors, including economic data, news events, and investor activity.

Market sentiment: Market participants' psychology and sentiment greatly influence market developments. When investors are enthusiastic about the future of an asset or the market as a whole, they tend to buy more, pushing prices higher. When sentiment goes negative, selling pressure can cause price drops.

Fundamental Factors: Fundamental analysis identifies economic, financial, and industry-specific elements that influence market developments. For example, good company earnings, favorable economic indicators, or government measures that promote economic growth can all contribute to bullish trends, whilst negative causes might lead to bearish trends.

Technical analysis: uses charts, patterns, and indicators to assess market trends. Traders employ tools like moving averages, trend-lines, and oscillators to confirm and forecast price changes. Technical analysts believe that historical price patterns can provide clues about future price movements.

Market participants: Retail investors, institutional investors, traders, and speculators can all affect market developments. Large institutional investors, such as mutual funds and hedge funds, can have a considerable impact on asset values when they acquire or sell large quantities.

News and events: Corporate earnings reports, economic data releases, geopolitical happenings, and central bank statements can impact market movements and patterns. Positive news can fuel bullish trends, whilst negative news can exacerbate bearish trends.

Chapter 4

Market participants and their impact

The foreign exchange market is populated by a wide range of participants, from tiny retail investors and beginning traders to huge hedge funds and commercial banks.

While there are many market participants with various goals and motives, we can generally categorize them to better understand how the FX market works.

The foreign currency market (FX) is the world's largest financial market. Banks, commercial companies, hedge funds, central banks, and individual speculators all participate and trade currencies on a regular basis for both speculative and hedging reasons.

Market Participant Market

See below for a list of the major participants who trade in the foreign currency market every day.

- Commercial banks
- Hedge funds
- Real money
- Retail traders
- Sovereign wealth funds
- Prime brokers
- Retail brokers
- Private trading firms
- Money transfer/remittance companies
- Commercial organizations

Participants in the Foreign Exchange Market

Commercial banks

Commercial banks are among the most prominent players in the foreign exchange market. They trade on their own behalf while simultaneously offering a way for their clients to participate in the market. They are vital for supplying liquidity and serve as the currency market's backbone.

Commercial banks not only assist their customers' trades, but they also speculate in the market. These desks are known as "proprietary trading desks," and the goal of the prop traders is to make a profit for their bank. Following the 2008 financial crisis, banks became more risk conservative, and prop trading declined. However, it can still be found in banks, particularly in nations with fewer regulatory limitations.

Commercial banks are among the most knowledgeable market participants, owing to their infrastructure, the quantity of cash available, and, perhaps most crucially, their knowledge of the market. Commercial banks might see a lot of money moving through the market, from central banks to hedge funds and investment firms. This information provides them with a significant advantage.

Hedge Funds

Hedge funds are the most notable speculators. While there are other forms of hedge funds, the two most active in the FX market are global macro funds and currency funds. Macro funds trade in a wide range of global markets, whereas currency funds seek out chances in the foreign exchange market. Hedge funds can manage large positions in the market and are significant participants.

Real money

'Real money' refers to investment funds that do not use leverage. These are typically pension and mutual funds that handle huge sums of money and use the FX market for transactions involving foreign securities. For example, purchasing a big number of UK stocks on the London Stock Exchange necessitates the purchase of the local currency, in this case, the Pound Sterling.

Retail traders

Individual traders often enter the market through a retail broker, although they may also utilize a prime broker if they have the requisite cash. Given the minimal amount of money required to create a trading account, retail traders can use leverage.

The scale of global retail trading is difficult to measure, however according to the Bank of International Settlements' most recent study in April 2019, retail traders exchanged $201 million. Volumes have been continuously increasing, and this trend is unlikely to reverse soon, as the currency market remains very appealing to individual traders.

Sovereign wealth funds

State-owned investment funds oversee the country's finances and invest them in a variety of markets. They are typically found in countries with huge inflows of foreign currency, such as Qatar from selling natural gas or Kuwait from selling oil. Sovereign wealth funds control substantial sums of money, thus their operations can have a significant impact on the forex market.

Prime brokers

Companies that provide liquidity, leverage, and support services to other market participants. Most large banks have prime brokerage operations, however there are also non-bank prime brokers operating in the industry. Prime brokers' clients are typically other institutional participants, but an individual trader may utilize a PB if he meets the broker's requirements.

Retail Brokers

Individual forex traders can gain access to the foreign exchange market through brokerage businesses. They could be market makers, STP brokers, or ECNs. Market makers take the other side of all customer deals, functioning primarily as dealers rather than brokers.

STP (straight-through-processing) brokers send the majority or all of their orders directly to the market, whereas an ECN allows you to trade with a variety of other players while the broker has no conflicts of interest.

Proprietary trading firms

Firms hire individual traders to trade the company's money and pay them a percentage of the profits they make. The trader can benefit from professional tools that would be prohibitively expensive to obtain on their own, a network of fellow professional traders, and capital allocation that can easily approach seven-figure sums for successful traders.

Money transfer and remittance companies

Companies that specialize in money transfers have been able to obtain significant market share over the last ten years.

This was mostly driven by digitalization and increased consumer awareness. They frequently outperform traditional banks' exchange rates, and considering that remittances from foreign workers have a significant impact on the economies of many developing countries, their importance is expanding. Money transfer firms typically do not engage in speculative trading.

Commercial companies

This group comprises a variety of corporations, such as international corporations and exporters/importers. Their primary purpose is not to earn from currency trading, but rather to hedge their currency risk or obtain the foreign currency required to pay their employees in other countries and so on.

Governments and Central Banks

Central banks intervene in the market when their currency gets excessively strong or too weak, causing problems for the domestic economy. This applies to all exchange-rate regimes, including floating, pegged, and fixed.

Who controls the currency market

The foreign exchange market is decentralized, and no organization regulates it. However, commercial banks act as market makers, whereas central banks have tremendous authority and can affect the market.

Generally, the FX market is too large for any single participant to manage.

For example, if a hedge fund decided to acquire $5 billion of GBP/USD at market pricing, the currency pair would most likely rise solely as a result.

However, because this is one of the most frequently traded currency pairings, the impact of this transaction will be short-term.

Furthermore, it is not in the best interests of market participants to move the market in this manner because it not only makes implementation more difficult but also betrays what they are doing. It is significantly easier for a hedge fund to keep a huge FX position hidden if it was built up over time rather than by making a massive trade all at once.

Chapter 5

The psychology behind market structure

Emotional discipline and market structure

As any seasoned trader will tell you, potential success in the market is not only about having the appropriate plan, but also about establishing two crucial qualities: discipline and patience in trading.

Discipline

In trading, discipline is the ability to constantly adhere to your trading plan and regulations. It entails avoiding impulsive emotional decisions and instead using a methodical approach that may assist you in managing risks and capturing potential benefits.

A disciplined trader is one who can control their impulses, stay focused, and avoid letting emotions distort their judgment.

Let us look at an example of discipline in action. Imagine someone has a string of winning deals and becomes overconfident. Instead of following their risk management approach, they considerably raise their position size on a high-risk trade in the hopes of making even more money. However, the market turned against them, resulting in enormous losses due to their lack of discipline.

Patience

Patience in trading refers to the capacity to wait for prospective chances rather than hurry into trades due to fear of missing out (FOMO). A patient trader realizes that the market may provide prospective chances, but attempting to seize every single one may result in bad decision-making.

Being patient entails waiting for opportunities, verifying that they correspond with your trading plan, and entering transactions with a calm and cool attitude.

Consider a circumstance in which you've been following a particular stock for a while but it hasn't moved significantly. A patient trader may wait for the stock price to reach a level consistent with their analysis and entry criteria. An eager trader, on the other hand, may enter the transaction too soon, raising the risk of losing money.

What might be called the right trading mindset

To gain discipline and patience in trading, you must establish the proper trading mindset. Here are some important characteristics of a trader with the appropriate mindset:

Realistic expectations:

Remember that trading is not a quick or easy way to get rich. Set achievable goals. Learn to accept both prospective rewards and losses, and constantly assess whether you can afford to lose.

Emotional Control:

Improve your capacity to regulate emotions such as fear and greed. Emotions might drive us to act without thinking, resulting in unwise decisions. Always take the time to assess the situation and make an informed conclusion.

Acceptance of unpredictability:

Recognize that the market is unpredictable, and not every trade has promise.

Continuous Learning:

Continue to be curious and committed to learning. Markets evolve, and traders must adjust to shifting conditions.

Confidence, not Overconfidence:

Confidence is important, but overconfidence can be harmful. Make your selections based on strong analysis and data.

How to Trade With Patience

Trading with patience entails a series of strategic steps that might help you stay disciplined and wait for future opportunities.

Stick to your trading plan.

You may have a well-defined trading strategy with specific entry and exit points. Follow it, avoiding deviations due to emotions or market noise.

Set realistic targets.

Avoid chasing unrealistic profit targets, which may cause you to take needless risks. Aim for consistency and create attainable goals each time.

Use stop loss orders:

Implement stop-loss orders to help protect your funds from major losses. This approach allows you to terminate a losing trade before it depletes your money.

Avoid overtrading.

Limit the number of deals you execute each day or week. Overtrading can cause weariness and lower the quality of your selections.

Wait for the confirmation:

Before making a trade, you can look for clues from technical indicators, price activity, or fundamental analysis.

How to Improve Discipline in Trading

Improving discipline is a continuous process that takes devotion and self-awareness. Here are some practical methods to improve your trading discipline:

Maintain a trading journal.

Keep meticulous records of all your trades, including entry and exit positions, reasoning for the trade, and emotional state. Keep reading through your journal for potential ways to improve.

Analyze your mistakes.

Accept that trading involves making mistakes. Instead than focusing on losses, consider what went wrong and how to avoid such mistakes in the future.

Create a trading routine.

Create a daily routine that involves pre-market analysis, personal research performance, setting alarms, and sticking to your strategy. A planned schedule may help you concentrate and avoid distractions.

Take breaks:

Long-term trading can cause weariness and a loss of discipline. Take regular breaks to cleanse your thoughts and keep a fresh viewpoint.

Crowd Psychology and the Market Cycle

Market Psychology

Market psychology is the theory that a market's movements mirror (or are influenced by) its players' emotional states. It is one of the key themes in behavioral economics, an interdisciplinary area that studies the different factors that influence economic decisions.

Many people feel that emotions are the primary cause of financial market fluctuations. And the overall fluctuation in investor opinion is what causes the so-called psychological market cycles.

In a nutshell, market sentiment refers to investors' and traders' general perceptions of an asset's price activity. A bullish trend is defined as a positive market sentiment and persistent price increases. A bear market is the antithesis of a bull market, in which prices continue to fall.

As a result, sentiment is comprised of the individual opinions and feelings of all traders and investors in a financial market. Another way to think about it is as an average of the total sentiment of market players.

However, like with any organization, no single viewpoint is totally dominant. According to market psychology theories, an asset's price fluctuates frequently in response to the general market attitude, which is likewise volatile. Otherwise, executing a successful transaction would be far more difficult.

In practice, when the market rises, it is usually due to an improved attitude and confidence among traders. A favorable market sentiment leads demand to rise and supply to fall. As a result, rising demand may lead to an even stronger attitude. Similarly, a significant decline tends to create a negative sentiment, reducing demand while increasing available supply.

How do emotions change across market cycles

In an Upward trend

All markets experience cycles of expansion and recession. When a market is expanding (in a bull market), there is a sense of optimism, belief, and greed. Typically, these are the primary emotions that drive considerable purchasing activity.

It is extremely typical to witness a cyclical or retroactive effect during market cycles.

For example, as prices rise, sentiment improves, which drives the market farther higher.

Sometimes a tremendous sense of greed and belief overtakes the market, causing a financial bubble to arise. In such a case, many investors become irrational, losing sight of the asset's true value and purchasing it solely because they believe the market will continue to increase.

They become greedy and overexcited by market movement, hoping to profit. As the price becomes overextended to the upside, the local top is formed. In general, this is regarded as the point of most financial danger.

In such circumstances, the market may go sideways for a while as assets are progressively unloaded. This is also called the distribution step. However, other cycles lack a definite distribution stage, and the downturn begins shortly after the peak is attained.

On a Downtrend

When the market begins to turn the other way, the euphoria rapidly turns to complacency, as many traders refuse to realize that the uptrend has ended. As prices continue to fall, market mood quickly turns negative. It frequently includes feelings of fear, denial, and panic.

In this context, we might define anxiety as the point at which investors begin to question why the price is falling, which eventually leads to the denial stage.

The denial period is characterized by feelings of unacceptance. Many investors refuse to sell their losing investments, either because "it's too late to sell" or because they feel "the market will come back soon."

However, as prices fall even further, the wave of selling intensifies. At this time, anxiety and panic frequently result in market capitulation (when investors give up and sell their assets around the local low).

The slump eventually comes to an end as volatility declines and the market stabilizes. Typically, the market moves sideways before feelings of hope and optimism return. This sideways era is often referred to as the accumulation stage.

How do investors apply market psychology

Understanding market psychology assist traders in entering and exiting positions at more advantageous moments. The market's general attitude is counterproductive: the best financial opportunity (for a buyer) frequently occurs when most people are depressed and the market is at its lowest point. In contrast, the largest level of financial danger frequently occurs when the bulk of market players are ecstatic and overconfident.

Thus, some traders and investors attempt to read a market's attitude in order to identify the various stages of its psychological cycles.

Ideally, they would utilize this information to buy when prices are low (panic) and sell when prices are high (greed). In practice, however, identifying these ideal positions is rarely a simple task. What appears to be a local bottom (support) may not hold, resulting in even lower lows.

Technical Analysis and Market Psychology

It is simple to look back on market cycles and see how the broader mentality changed. Analyzing past data reveals which activities and decisions would have yielded the highest profits.

However, understanding how the market changes over time is much more difficult, as is predicting what will happen next. Many investors use technical analysis (TA) to predict where the market will move.

In some ways, TA indicators can be seen of as tools for assessing the market's psychological state. For example, the Relative Strength Index (RSI) indicator may indicate that an asset is overbought due to a strong positive market sentiment (e.g., excessive greed).

The MACD is another indicator that may be used to identify the various psychological stages of a market cycle. In summary, the relationship between its lines may signal when market momentum shifts (e.g., buying force weakens).

The Psychology of Support and Resistance

The psychology behind support and resistance levels in trading stems from market players' collective behavior and emotions, which influence supply and demand for a certain asset. Understanding this mentality is critical for traders to make sound decisions when trading near these crucial price levels.

Support levels:

Psychological Comfort:

A support level is a price at which buyers are willing to purchase an asset. This level is frequently seen as a psychological comfort zone, in which traders believe the asset is undervalued and anticipate to see purchasing interest.

FOMO (Fear of Missing Out)

Traders may be concerned about missing out on an opportunity to buy an asset at a lower price. As the price approaches a support level, more people become interested in buying, creating demand and keeping the price from falling further.

Market Memory:

Support levels might also be influenced by past price trends. Traders frequently look at previous support levels where the price has reversed, resulting in a self-fulfilling prophesy as traders recall these levels and predict price rebounds.

Resistance levels:

Psychological resistance:

A resistance level is a price at which sellers are willing to enter the market and sell an asset. Traders view this level as a psychological resistance point, when they believe the asset is overvalued and expect selling pressure.

Profit-Taking

When the price hits a resistance level, traders who have previously acquired the asset may decide to take profits. This activity increases the asset's supply, which puts downward pressure on the price.

Fear of Loss:

Traders may become more cautious when the price approaches a resistance level, worrying that the asset will reverse or fall in value. This prudence may lead to more people selling at resistance.

Market Memory:

Historical price behavior at resistance levels, like that of support, informs traders' judgments. They may recollect previous reversals at resistance, creating a self-fulfilling prophecy.

Overall, it is crucial to realize that support and resistance levels are not fixed and can be breached. Traders must be aware of the possibility of false breakouts or crashes.

The psychology of support and resistance levels is a critical component of technical analysis. Traders utilize these levels to determine probable entry and exit points and to manage risk. Successful trading requires not only understanding these psychological dynamics, but also having a well-defined trading strategy and risk management plan to negotiate the market's intricacies.

Chapter 6

Market structure in different time frame

Market structure is the most basic form of price movement in the market. It consists of basic chart support and resistance levels, as well as swing highs and swing lows. These are levels that are immediately identifiable and persist until they do not. Market structure is a trend-following tool that traders use to track how an asset moves. Ranges cover bullish, bearish, and neutral moves.

Top-down Analysis

Top-down analysis is a technique for gaining a thorough picture of market dynamics by analyzing several time periods and market elements simultaneously.

Starting with larger time frames and drilling in on lesser details allows us to acquire a broad view of market trend and significant regions at all levels.

Why Combine Multiple Timeframes

Top three reasons for combining several time frames:

Overcome Directional Confusion:

Analyzing larger time periods aids in overcoming directional uncertainty. When the market appears choppy and unclear in shorter time frames, zooming out to higher time frames enables traders to rapidly detect market trend and direction. This enables traders to enter short positions with confidence in the shorter time frames.

Increasing Accuracy:

Checking higher time frame key levels before placing a transaction allows us to determine how much room we have before entering a higher time frame supply or demand area. This understanding enables us to define goals, reduce losses, and avoid unnecessary risks.

Optimizing trade entries:

Analyzing several time frames allows us to identify optimal trading entry and exit points. By seeking for confirmation in shorter time periods, we can enter trades at cheaper prices, limit the possibility of false signals, and boost our confidence in our research.

Top-Down Analysis Technique

Now that we understand the need of a multi-time frame analysis, let's walk through a top-down analysis technique step by step.

1. Identify major market structure levels using higher time frames (weekly and daily).

2. Analyze market direction, supply and demand, order blocks, liquidity zones, and trading opportunities using four and one hour time frames.

3. Use 15- and 5-minute time limits for additional confirmations and entries.

Intraday market structure.

Forex Day Trading

Forex day trading is a short-term trading method that involves purchasing and selling currency pairs on the same trading day. Traders typically place a number of forex trades every day and close them out at the end of the trading day, rather than holding positions overnight. Price swings in liquid currency pairs can present several chances for day traders, therefore they typically seek out currency pairs that are both liquid and volatile.

Forex day trading entails responding to short-term variations in the values of currency pairings, which necessitates control, focus, discipline, and the ability to stick to a trading plan.

Forex Day Trading Strategies

When it comes to the foreign currency market, traders need be aware with various trading methods. Typical forex trading techniques include technical analysis, fundamental analysis, or a combination of the two. Forex day traders will utilize this study to determine when to purchase and sell currency pairs.

Forex day trading may necessitate the use of multiple strategies. Because market conditions change on a daily basis, traders should be prepared to adjust their strategy, particularly during periods of high market liquidity.

Forex news day trading strategy.

Traders will want to stay current on the latest trading news releases in the short term. Knowing what's going on in the markets can help traders prepare for prospective trading decisions ahead of time, as well as plan their trading goals and techniques for the day.

Central bank statements, interest rate increases, and other data releases are all crucial economic indicators that can have an impact on currency markets, thus day traders must stay on top of major economic announcements and news events.

Trend trading day trading strategy.

Trend trading is another prominent strategy used by FX day traders. This entails analyzing longer-term charts to identify a trend. Once the general trend has been identified, traders will look at a chart with a shorter timeframe for trends that are heading in the same direction.

Momentum day trading strategy

Momentum trading is another popular strategy for FX day trading. This strategy searches for big price changes accompanied by a high volume of trading in the direction of the move. Momentum trading entails being able to wait for the optimal time to begin a position.

Breakouts Day Trading Strategy

Breakout trading is a prominent forex day trading technique that includes waiting for large market changes. These large movements might be caused by changes in a country's economic data. They might occur abruptly or following anticipated economic statements. Breakout trading involves waiting for prices to break through important price support and resistance levels, signifying the beginning of a trend. The trader would then open a position in the direction they believe prices would move.

Identifying and trading forex breakouts is an effective approach for individuals who stay current on economic and political news.

Swing Trading

A swing trade is one that is kept for more than a single trading session or day.

A swing trade is a trade that lasts from a number of days to several months, in order to profit from an expected price move in the traded item.

Why is it called swing trading

The increase/decrease of price in an instrument over time rarely occurs in a straight 'line' up or down, but rather in 'waves' in which price travels quickly in one direction and then rests before moving again in the same direction.

These 'waves' are responsible for bullish or bearish patterns, which can last anywhere from a few hours to several years depending on the time range.

Every time that price starts a pullback or starts a new move after a pullback creates so-called swing points, and thus, as a swing trader, you're looking to get in as close as possible to a swing low in the trend and exit as close as possible to a swing high to capture as much of the trend move as possible, which is why it's called swing trading.

Swing trading advantages and disadvantages

Swing trading has advantages than day trading on lower time frames, but there are also drawbacks, which we will discuss below.

Advantages of Swing Trading

Swing trading has various features that make it a popular trading strategy for many people. Swing trading has several major advantages, including the following:

Time

Day trading may be particularly time-consuming because traders must constantly check the markets and their positions. Swing trading allows traders to periodically check their positions, giving them more time to analyze markets and develop their approach.

Day traders typically devote their entire day to this activity, making swing trading appealing to traders with less time at their disposal.

Emotional Control:

Day trading can be time-consuming and demanding. Not every trader can remain calm when pressed to make quick decisions, and such traders may profit from swing trading, which is less emotionally exhausting than day trading.

Less Noise:

The shorter the timescale, the higher the noise. Trading on a 5-minute chart generates a large number of signals, making it much more difficult to separate the good from the poor.

Reduced transaction costs:

Every deal incurs a spread, commission charge, or both. The fewer frequently someone trades, the lower their overall transaction costs.

Trend and Counter-trend Trading:

Swing traders can either follow the current trend or profit from short-term reversals.

Disadvantages of swing trading

Traders should be mindful of the following challenges when swing trading:

Risk of unexpected events:

The danger of an unexpected market occurrence is always present, but swing traders are more exposed to it because they frequently hold positions overnight, as opposed to day traders. Unexpected events can produce considerable price changes and market gaps, which may result in losses.

Volatility:

Swing traders are more vulnerable to short-term volatility than position traders, who hold positions for months and are better prepared for markets to turn against them.

Timing:

Finding the right entry and exit opportunities can be more challenging than day trading. Swing traders are also more likely to modify their stop-loss and take-profit levels, which takes additional effort and time.

A number of trading opportunities:

Swing traders frequently trade on larger timeframe charts, which naturally results in less signals and trading possibilities.

Trading Psychology:

While swing trading gives traders more time to plan and ponder than day trading, which requires quick choices, it can be difficult to keep positions open for an extended period of time. Traders are more likely to doubt themselves and make mistakes when their position lasts several days rather than a few hours.

Costs:

While swing traders pay lower commissions and spreads, their swap costs are larger since they frequently hold positions for longer periods of time. Swap expenses can easily pile up if not well monitored, reducing the trader's profit and loss.

Types of Swing Trading Strategies

Trend Following:

Traders recognize and exploit market trends. They adhere to the premise that price movements tend to stay in the direction of the current trend. The idea is to capitalize on the trend as soon as possible. To confirm the direction, you'll need to know how to use indicators like moving averages.

Breakout Trading:

The market fluctuates between support (lower point) and resistance (upper point) levels. This is termed a "range." However, when prices break through this range, it is referred to as breakout trading. Basically, the price begins to rally. Technical indicators such as Bollinger Bands and the Relative Strength Index (RSI) can be used to determine whether the breakout is a strong or false signal.

Pullback Trading:

Buyers and sellers attempt to drive prices in opposite directions. Even if the trend is favorable, you may see minor pullbacks or corrections. These are modest price reversals that provide an excellent opportunity to enter the trade. Use Fibonacci retracement levels to determine pullbacks.

Reversal Trading:

Reversal traders take positions in the opposite direction of the current trend. This is a dangerous technique, therefore make sure to use tight stop-loss orders.

Momentum Trading:

This method is all about leveraging momentum. Swing traders that utilize this method often have shorter holding periods and want quick gains.

Top Markets and Instruments for Swing Trading

Swing trading is applicable to any type of instrument, including stocks, commodities, and forex.

When selecting your instrument, bear the following in mind:

Liquidity:

Choose an instrument with high liquidity. The term "liquidity" refers to how easy or difficult it is to liquidate a position without causing significant price slippage. High liquidity allows you to easily initiate and exit trades.

Volatility:

Swing trading thrives on price fluctuations. Forex pairs such as EUR/USD and GBP/JPY are considered volatile. This means you'll see a lot of highs and lows on the charts, providing you plenty of opportunities for swing trading.

Trading Costs:

Be aware of trading charges such as spreads. The "spread" is the difference between the bid price (the most a buyer is ready to pay) and the asking price (the least a seller is willing to take). Commissions and overnight finance charges are additional expenditures to consider. Also, make sure to compare pricing from several brokers.

How to Get Started with Swing Trading

To successfully execute swing trading, use these recommendations and best practices:

Define your trading goal.

Set a definite, quantifiable, and realistic goal to help you stay focused and disciplined. This should include profit targets, annual returns, and growth goals.

Risk Tolerance:

Do not trade without first determining your risk tolerance. Decide how much of your capital you are ready to risk on each transaction. This will assist you in managing your emotions.

Capital Allocation:

Never risk more than 1-3% of your whole capital on a single trade. Also, diversify your funds across numerous trades to spread the risk and mitigate the effects of losses.

Set the entry and exit rules.

Set specified trading conditions, including take-profit and stop-loss thresholds.

If you regularly follow these criteria, you will approach each transaction in a systematic and disciplined manner.

Continuously evaluate your performance.

Keep a trading notebook to record the results of each trade, as well as the entry and exit points and reasoning behind them. Over time, you'll be able to identify patterns in your transactions and learn from your failures.

Master Psychology:

Emotional control is crucial for trading. So be patient while you wait for the best trade setups. Resist the urge to pursue deals. Mindfulness can help you avoid taking unnecessary risks motivated by greed or fear. View losses as learning opportunities.

Thank you for purchasing this book, go through other of my materials on amazon store.

Happy trading!

Link to video access of this course and other free forex video course on next page.

Thank you for purchasing this book, you can follow the below link for the video access for this book

Access Link to Advanced Market Structure Video Course

https://www.youtube.com/playlist?list=PLsr29W8GhQK 3rF9ndcxrpHeK2TxiKnWiH

Link to Other Video Course

subscribepage.io/freeforexcourse